1

THE PRINCIP LES OF GETTING MONEY

ULTIMATE GUIDES IN MAKING MONEY

ROBERT L. GIARDINA

4

Disclaimer Note

This book is only intended to provide knowledge that is relevant. Every effort has been made to provide accurate, current, trustworthy, and comprehensive information..

TABLE OF CONTENT

DO NOT EXCEED YOUR BUSINESS

LEARN SOMETHING VALUE-ADDED

LEAD WITH HOPE, BUT DON'T BE TOO VISIONARY

DON'T DISTRIBUTE YOUR POWERS

BE SYMPATHETIC

SEEK NEWS IN THE PAPERS

WARNING: "EXTERNAL OPERATIONS"

NOT WITHOUT SECURITY; DO NOT ENDORSE

PROMOTE YOUR BUSINESS

DON'T READ THE OTHER SIDE"

BE HUMAN AND GRATEFUL TO YOUR CUSTOMERS

THINK CHARITABLY

AVOID BLAB

DON'T LOSE YOUR INTEGRITY

INTRODUCTION

The purpose of this book is to talk about creating money, to look at how common it is among individuals as a goal, and to look at the moral standards attained by those who actively pursue getting money.

Most men share a desire to be financially successful. In some form, whether stronger or weaker, it occupies almost everyone's attention. How far does this desire develop into a goal or object in our lives, and how much of a worthy goal is this?

The typical money-maker, as we typically imagine

him or her, is a
constrictive, grasping,
selfish person who has
chosen to uphold lower
ideals over higher ones. He
or she is frequently
tempted, and may always
be tempted, to use illegal
means to further his goals.
His objectives are designed
to conflict with the
exercise of particular
virtues. Thus, we compare

and contrast profit and
patriotism, self-enrichment
and altruism, receiving
what the law permits for
others and honesty, and
becoming preoccupied
with acquisition and family
love. Now, these
comparisons obviously
show nothing more than
the fact that making money
is and would be a vicious
aim if pursued regardless

of these virtues, and it is quite possible to respond that thinking about one's country, being charitable, loving one's family, etc., must in themselves motivate one to earn and to save. The phrase "The love of money is the source of all evil" suggests a solemn devotion to acquisition that may readily be questioned. Aside from this, it is undeniable that, despite the conflicting views on the matter, the pursuit of wealth is frequently seen as being in opposition to societal virtues.

The purpose of this essay is to talk about creating money, to look at how common it is among individuals as a goal, and to look at the moral standards attained by those

who actively pursue
getting money.

DON'T MISS YOUR OCCASION

The stylish strategy for a
youthful man just starting
out in life is to choose a
profession that appeals to

his interests the most. In this aspect, parents and guardians are constantly far too careless. Fathers constantly use expressions like these, for illustration" My five sons are boys. Billy, John, Tom, and Dick will come clergymen, attorneys, croakers , and growers, independently." He also makes his way into the city to look around and decide what to do with Sammy. Sammy, I see watch-timber is an awful refined business; I suppose I'll make you a goldsmith, he says when he gets home. He does this anyhow of Sam's intelligence or essential propensities.

Without distrust, each of us was born for a good

reason. Both our faces and our smarts are incredibly different. Some people have a strong dislike to outfit, while others are born naturalmechanics.However, you will snappily notice that two or three of them are" whittling" down at some creative gimmick, thrashing with cinches or intricate outfit, If you gather a group of ten-time-old boys. Their father was unfit to find a toy that would appeal to them like a mystification when they were just five times old. Although the other eight or nine guys have varied aptitudes, they're both natural mechanics. I fall into the ultimate order; I've never loved mechanisms in the least; rather, I've an illogical abomination of intricate technology. I norway had the creativity to sculpt a cider valve similar that it wouldn't blunder. I was not suitable to understand the workings of a brume machine or produce a pen that I could write with. The youth might be able to disassemble and assemble a watch after five or seven

internships if a man tried
to turn me into a
watchmaker, but he'd
spend the rest of his life
working hard and changing
every defense to put off his
tasks and waste time. He
finds watchmaking
unwelcome.

 Man can not prosper
unless he engages in the
vocation that's most suited

to his unique gift and that's meant for him by nature. I am relieved to suppose that the utmost people do discover their ideal profession. Still, from the blacksmith on up(or down) to the dominie, we encounter individuals who have misknowled their calling. You may have seen attorneys, croakers

, and clergymen who were more suited by nature for the anvil or the lapstone, as well as that amazing linguist known as the" educated blacksmith," who should have become a language educator.

CHOOSE THE RIGHT PLACE

After choosing the ideal profession, you must be conservative to make the suitable position choice. They claim it takes a genius to" know how to run a hotel," therefore you might have been made for the job. Indeed if you run a hotel flawlessly and can comfortably accommodate 500 people per day, the placement of your home in a remote community without access to either public transportation or a road would be your death. It's also vital that you avoid opening an establishment in an area where there are formerly sufficient resources to supply all demand. I can suppose of a case that exemplifies this content. I visited the" penny shows" in 1858 when visiting London with an English familiarity while we were walking down Holborn. Huge cartoons depicting the fascinating oddities available to be seen" all for a penny" were displayed outdoors. I said," Let us go in also," since I was a little in the" show line" myself. The notorious showman suddenly appeared before us, and he snappily established himself as the most intelligent person I had ever encountered in that field. We set it up to accept some of the implausible tales he told us about his bearded ladies, Albinos, and Armadillos, but we decided that it was" better to believe it than look after the confirmation." He

ultimately contended with
us to pay attention to some
wax statues before
displaying a large
collection of the flirt and
filthy wax figures possible
to us. Since the Deluge,
they appeared as though
they had not seen water.

" What about your statues
is so awful?" I queried.

" These figures are not
Madam Barbara
waxworks, sir; they are all
covered in chased, tinsel.

and reduplication jewels,
and copied from
delineations and prints, I
pray you not to speak so
satirically, he said. Sir,
mine were snared from
life. When you look at one
of those figurines, you

might imagine that you are seeing a real person."

 I casually glanced over them and noticed one labeled" Henry VIII." Curious because it recalled Calvin Edson, the living shell, I asked" Do you call that" Henry the Eighth?"" easily, joe. It was taken from life at Hampton Court, on such a day, by

31

express order of his
majesty," he said.

  still, he would have
revealed the time of day;
rather, I asked, "If I had
refused."

  He responded," Why, you
would be thin and limp if
you sat there as long as he
has..

These arguments could not be refuted. Let's go outside; don't tell him who I am; I show the white feather; he beats me, I said to my English friend.

As we approached the door, he followed us and, upon spotting the unruly crowd outside, yelled," Ladies and Gentlemen, I pray to direct your

attention to the decent
nature of my guests,"
pointing to us as we left. A
few days later, I called him
and introduced myself. I
said

" My friend, although you
are a great showman, you
have chosen a poor point."

This is true, joe; I feel as
if all of my vents have

been wasted, but what can
I do? he retorted.

You can travel to
America, I said. You can
use all of your faculties
there, and there will be a
cornucopia of rooms for
you to move around in
America. I'll hire you for
two times, after which you
can leave on your own
song.

He accepted my offer and stayed in my New York Museum for two times. After that, he repositioned to New Orleans where he operated a summertime traveling entertainment business. He is now valued at $70 000, just because he made the perfect career choice and attained the ideal position. The saying"

Three removes are as dreadful as a fire" is an ancient one, yet when a man is in the fire, it doesn't really count how soon or how constantly he removes.

AVOID LOAN

Young men just starting out in life should refrain

from accruing debt. Many effects can bring a person down as much as debt. It's a slave-like situation to be placed in, yet we see numerous youthful men who are just coming out of their" teens" who are running up debt." Look at this I've gotten trusted for a new outfit of clothes," he tells a friend. Although this is constantly the case, if he

manages to pay and is
latterly trusted formerly
more, he's developing a
habit that will keep him in
poverty for the rest of his
life. A man who's in debt
loses all sense of tone-
respect and comes to
nearly detest himself.
Working for a dead steed
is directly described as' '
murmuring and moaning
and working for what he

has eaten up or worn out"
since when he's asked to
pay, he has nothing to
show for his plutocrat. I do
not talk about business
possessors who buy and
sell on credit or consumers
who use credit to make a
profit on a purchase." John,
no way get trusted; but if
thee gets trusted for
anything, let it before
manure,' for it'll help thee

pay it back again," the old
Quaker advised his planter
son.

 Beecher recommended
youthful men to adopt
plutocrats, indeed if it was
only a little sum, to buy
land in pastoral areas. He
asserts that if a youthful
man just incurs debt to buy
some land and the lawyer
gets wedded, none of these

two conduct will keep him moral. To a certain extent, this might be safe, but you should avoid going into debt to pay for your clothes, food, and drink. Some families make the unwise decision to use credit at" the stores," which leads to frequent purchases of particulars that may be avoided.

Saying" I've been trusted for sixty days, and if I do not have the plutocrat, the creditor will not suppose doubly about it" is all veritably well and good. Creditors are the only class of individualities in the world with similar positive recollections. You must make payment once the sixty days have passed. You'll transgress your word and presumably start telling falsehoods if you do not pay. To pay it off, you can come up with an explanation or dodge debt away, but doing so simply makes the effects worse for you.

 Horatio, the apprentice boy, was a seductive but sluggish youthful man." Horatio, have you ever seen a crawler?" his master said. I guess I have, he muttered." I am sure you noway passed one, so you must have run into him also," the" master" remarked." " Now, my youthful friend, you agreed to pay me; you haven't done it. You must give me your note," your creditor will say as they approach or catch you. When you apply interest on a note, it incontinently starts to work against you;" it is a dead steed." The creditor goes to bed at night and wakes up the coming morning having made further plutocrats than when he went to bed since his interest rose, but while you sleep, you come poorer because interest is accruing against you.

plutocrat is analogous to
fire in certain ways; it
makes an amazing menial
but a dreadful master. The
worst type of servility will
drag you down when it's
learning you and when
interest is steadily piling
up against you. Still, if you
make plutocrats work for
you, you'll have the world's
most pious menial. There's

no" eye- menial" then.
Nothing insensible or amp
will serve as dependably as
plutocrats when it's
invested and duly secured.
It functions day and night,
in dry or wet conditions.

 I was born in Connecticut,
a state with strict blue laws
where it was indeed stated
that" they punished a man
for kissing his woman

on Sunday." still, these fat old Bluenoses would have thousands of bones
 earning interest and would be worth a certain quantum on Saturday night. On Sunday, they would attend church and fulfill all of their Christian scores. As a result of their plutocrat earning interest all day Sunday, as needed by law, they would find

themselves far richer on Monday morning than they were on Saturday night.

 Avoid letting it work against you; if you do, you will not have any occasion of achieving success in life as it relates to plutocrats. The eccentric Virginian John Randolph allegedly declared in front of Congress,"Mr. Speaker,

I've set up the champion's gravestone pay as you go." In actuality, this is the closest an alchemist has ever come to the champion's gravestone.

MAINTAIN

Endure A joe must persist if he's on the correct road. This is important to note since there are some people who are" born tired" — lazy by nature, lacking in tone- reliance and tenacity. But as Davy Crockett noted, they may cultivate these traits.

" Flash back to this when I am gone. Be certain you are correct before moving on."

You must make this forward- allowing decision not to let the" horrors" of the" blues" retain you in order to allow your powers to be released in the fight for freedom.

How many people have come close to realizing their goals but, after losing stopgap in themselves, let

their guard down and let
the prize slip down?

It's really constantly true
what Shakespeare says

In mortal events, there's a
drift that, when ridden at
its crest, leads to wealth.

A stalwart hand will
stretch out in front of you
and take the prize if you

delay. A wise man once said," He who deals with a slack hand becomes poor; but the hand of the active makes rich."

tone- reliance is sometimes just another term for perseverance. numerous people are prone to seeing the worst aspects of life and borrowing problems. They're fitted to

being this way from birth.
also they seek advice
because they can not
calculate on themselves
and will be carried along
by one wind and blown by
another. You should not
count on success until you
can calculate solely on
yourself.

 Guys who endured fiscal
lapses and actually

committed themselves because they believed they would nowadays be suitable to recover from their mischance are men I've tête-à-tête known. I have, still, given people who have faced more severe fiscal challenges and have overcome them through sheer tenacity, helped by a strong conviction that they were acting justly and that Providence will" overcome evil with good." Any area of life will serve to illustrate this.

Still, both of whom attended West Point for their education, the former will thrive in his field while the latter will fail because of the perseverance principle. If

you compare two generals
who are inversely talented.
The yell" the adversary is
approaching, and they've
ordnance" is audible.

 The reluctant commander
asks," Got cannon?"

" Yes."

" Also stop each man."

The general of courage, perseverance, and tone-reliance, on the other hand, goes into battle with a will and, amid the clash of arms, the roaring of cannons, the mutters of the wounded, and the moans of the dying, you'll see this man persisting, going on, cutting and slashing his way through with unwavering determination,

60

inspiring his dog faces to deeds of valor.

Whatever you do, put your all into it.

Never leave a stone unturned and never put off for even a single hour what can be done just as well now. Work on it early in the morning and late at night, during the season and out of the season. The classic saying, "Whatever is worth doing at all, is worth doing well," is replete with truth and significance. Many men make a fortune by conducting their business fully, while their neighbors, who do it only partially, stay impoverished for the rest of their lives. For a firm to succeed, ambition, drive, industry, and perseverance are essential requirements.

Fortune never assists a man who does not help himself; it always favors the brave. It won't do to wait around as Mr. Micawber does for things to "turn up" in your life.

63

Since idleness promotes ill
habits and dresses a man in
rags, one of two things
typically "turns up" for
such men: the poorhouse
or the prison. The
impoverished, wasteful
vagrant remarks to the
wealthy:

"I have found that there is
enough money in the world
to support us all, if it were

split evenly. If this is done, we will all be happy together."

But if everyone responded in the same manner, it would be gone in two months. What would you do then'?

"Oh! Divide once more, and keep doing so, of course!"

I recently came across a story about a similar philosophical pauper who was expelled from a cheap boarding house because he couldn't pay the bill. Upon closer inspection, the roll of papers that were protruding from his coat pocket turned out to be his strategy for paying off the national debt of England without using a single penny. People must follow Cromwell's advice to "keep the powder dry" in addition to having faith in Providence. Put forth your fair share of effort if you want to achieve. Mahomet once overheard one of his weary followers say, "I shall lose my camel, and trust it to God," as they were camped out in the desert. The prophet responded, "No, no, not at all. Tie your camel, and put your trust in God." Do what you can for yourself, and leave the rest up to Providence, luck, or whatever you want to call it.

USE YOUR OWN PERSONAL EXERCISES AS A GUIDE.

The eyes of the employer are frequently more valuable than a dozen workers' worth of hands. An agent cannot, by nature, be as devoted to his employer as he is to himself. Many people who

69

are employers may recall
incidents where the best
workers have missed
crucial details that could
not have escaped their own
attention as an owner. No
man has the right to
assume that he will
succeed in life until he
fully comprehends his
industry, and no one can
fully comprehend his
industry unless he learns it

by personal application and experience. A man could become a manufacturer, but he would need to learn the many details of his industry personally. He would discover he would almost certainly make mistakes every day and would learn something new every day. And if he only pays attention to

them, these very mistakes
help him learn from his
experiences. He will
follow in the footsteps of
the Yankee tin-peddler,
who after being duped into
believing his goods were
of higher quality than they
actually were, declared:
"All right, there's a little
information to be acquired
every day; I will never be
duped in that way again."

Man buys his experience in this way, and if it isn't too expensive, it's the best sort.

I firmly believe that every man should be as knowledgeable about his industry as the French naturalist Cuvier. He was so knowledgeable about natural history that you could show him a bone or even a piece of a bone

from an animal that he had
never heard of before, and
using analogy, he would be
able to create a picture of
the thing the bone had
come from. His classmates
once made an attempt to
trick him. One of their
numbers was wrapped in a
cow skin and placed
beneath the professor's
desk as a fresh specimen.
Some of the pupils

questioned the philosopher about what animal it was when he entered the room. The animal abruptly yelled, "I am the devil, and I'm going to eat you." Cuvier's desire to categorize this species was only natural, and after closely inspecting it, he stated:

"Separated hoof; grazer! It is not possible."

He believed himself to be completely safe because he understood that an animal with a damaged hoof must consume grass, grain, or another type of plant and would not be motivated to eat flesh, either living or dead. In order to guarantee success, having a complete

76

understanding of your
industry is a must.

Be careful and brave was
one of the elder
Rothschild's maxims,
which seems to contradict
itself. Although it may
appear like a contradiction
in terms, the saying
actually has a lot of
insight. In actuality, it is a
shortened version of what I

already said. It means "you must be cautious when making ideas, yet brave when carrying them out." A man who is only cautious will never have the courage to seize the initiative and succeed, and a man who is only courageous is simply reckless and will inevitably fail. A man may go "on the change" and make $50,000 or $100,000 through stock trading in a single transaction. However, if someone is just brave without prudence, his success is purely accidental, and whatever success he has today, he will lose tomorrow. To ensure success, you need to be both cautious and brave.

Another dictum of the Rothschilds is, "Never deal with a bad man or a bad place." This means that you should never associate with someone or somewhere that is consistently unsuccessful because, even though a person may come across as honest and intelligent, if they consistently try something and fail, they must have some flaw or weakness that you are unable to detect.

There is no such thing as luck in the world. He may do so once in his life, but as far as pure luck is concerned, he is just as likely to lose it as to find it. There has never been a man who could go outside in the morning and find a purse full of gold in the street today, another tomorrow, and so on, day after day. Similar causes lead to similar effects. If a man uses the right strategies, "luck" will not stand in his way. There are reasons why he might not succeed, even though he might not be able to see them.

APPLY THE BEST MATERIALS

P than he was last. If, as he becomes more valuable, he requests an outrageous wage raise, let him go if you feel you can't function without him. Every time I have such an employee, I always let him go. First, to persuade him that his

position might be filled,
and second, because he is
useless if he believes he is
indispensable and cannot
be spared.

But if I could, I would
keep him so I could benefit
from his experience. The
brain is an essential
component of a worker.
Although there are bills
saying "Hands Wanted,"

"hands" are not very valuable without "heads." Mr. Beecher provides an example of this as follows:

"I have a pair of hands and one of my fingers thinks," the employee saves, before offering his services. The boss comments, "That is quite good." When a second man enters the room, he remarks, "He has

two fingers that think." Ah,
that's much better. An
additional caller, though,
claims that "all his fingers
and thumbs think." That is
even better. When
someone else finally
speaks, he or she declares,
"I have a brain that thinks;
I think all the time; I am a
thinking as well as a
working guy!" The thrilled

employer declares, "You are the man I want.

Men with brains and experience are consequently the most valuable and should not be easily parted with; it is preferable for them and for you to keep them, with periodic appropriate salary increases.

DO NOT EXCEED YOUR BUSINESS

Instead of pursuing their vocation and moving up in their firm after completing their business training or apprenticeship, young men frequently tell lies about doing nothing. What is the point of learning my trade or profession unless I establish myself? they ask. "I have learned my business, but I am not going to be a hireling."

"Do you have any initial capital?"

"No, but I'm having it anyhow."

How will you obtain it, I ask?

"I'll tell you this privately: I have a wealthy elderly aunt who is about to pass away. If she does not, I expect to locate a wealthy elderly man who will lend me a few thousand dollars

to get started. I will
succeed if I can just secure
the funding first."

There is no worse error
than for a young man to
think that using borrowed
money will help him
succeed. Why? Because
every man has had a
similar experience to Mr.
Astor, who claimed that
"accumulating his first

$1,000 was harder for him than all the subsequent millions that made up his huge wealth," Money is useless unless you have firsthand knowledge of its value. A boy who is given $20,000 and placed in business is likely to lose every dollar of it before becoming 18 years old. It's "easy come, easy go," just like purchasing a lottery

ticket and winning a
jackpot. He is unaware of
its worth because nothing
has value unless it requires
work. Without self-control,
economy, patience, and
perseverance, as well as
starting with capital that
you have not earned, you
are unlikely to succeed in
building up a significant
amount of wealth. There is
no class of people that is as

unaccommodating in regards to dying as these wealthy old people, and it is fortunate for the expectant heirs that it is so. Young men should be up and doing instead of "waiting for dead men's shoes." Nine out of 10 of the wealthy men in our society today were once poor boys with strong wills, work ethic, tenacity, thrift, and moral values. They progressed gradually, earned their own money, and stored it; this is the most effective approach to amass wealth. Stephen Girard was born a meager cabin lad and died with a net worth of $9 million. A.T. Stewart was an impoverished Irish boy who paid taxes on an annual income of

$1,500,000. Despite being a poor farm boy, John Jacob Astor passed away with a net worth of $20,000,000. Beginning his life by rowing a boat from Staten Island to New York, Cornelius Vanderbilt later gave our country a steamer for a million dollars and passed away with a fortune of fifty million dollars. The proverb states that "there is no royal way to study," and I would add that the same is true of "there is no royal road to prosperity." However, I believe there is a royal path to both. The path to learning is a regal one; it enables the student to develop his intellect and increase his knowledge base day by day, until, in the enjoyable process of

intellectual development,
he is able to solve the most
difficult problems, count
the stars, examine each
atom of the earth, and
measure the firmament.
This regal highway is the
only one that is worthwhile
taking .

NOTE:

- So in terms of money.
Continue with
confidence, learn the

laws, and most importantly, learn about human nature because "the proper study of mankind is man." You'll discover that as you develop your intellect and himuscles, your expanded experience will allow you to accumulate more and more principal every

day, which will grow
by interest and other
means until you reach a
state of independence.
Generally speaking,
you'll discover that
poor lads get rich and
rich boys get poor. For
instance, a wealthy guy
who passes away
leaves his family a
sizable estate. His two
eldest sons have

assisted him in accumulating his wealth, so they are aware of the importance of money and add to their inheritance. The various parts of the young children are given consideration, and the little ones are stroked on the head and reminded repeatedly throughout the day that they are affluent and don't need to work because they were born with everything they could possibly want. The young heir quickly realizes what that implies because he has the most luxurious clothes and toys, is overstuffed with sugary treats, was almost "killed with kindness," and is constantly patted and complimented as he moves from school to school. He starts to act haughtily and self-righteously, mistreats his professors, and carries everything with a high hand. He has never earned money, thus he has no idea what money is really worth, but he is an expert in the "golden spoon" industry. He "wines and dines" his impoverished college roommates by inviting them over. Due to his extravagant spending, he is encouraged and petted while also being referred to as a glorious excellent follower. Intent on having lots of "good times," he hosts his own hunting dinners, rides his own swift horses, and invites his friends to fetes and parties. He spends the night having fun and acting wild, and he sends his friends out with the well-known song, "We won't go home until morning." He convinces them to help him take down signs, remove gates from their hinges, and hurl them into horse ponds and backyards. He knocks them down, is brought to the jail, and happily pays the expenses if the police come and arrest them.

"Ah! What good is being wealthy if you can't enjoy yourself, my guys," he cries."

If you can't make a fool of yourself, he would more accurately state; nonetheless, he is "quick," despises slow things, and doesn't "see it." Young men who inherit large sums of money from others are nearly certain to lose whatever they have, and they often develop a variety of terrible habits that, in most cases, damage their health, finances, and moral character. In this nation, one generation follows another, and the current impoverished are either the second or third generation's richest people. Their knowledge propels them forward, they become wealthy, and they bequeath their young children great fortunes. These children, who were raised in luxury, lack experience and become impoverished; nevertheless, with time and experience, a new generation will emerge and amass wealth once more. As a result, "history repeats itself," and happy is the man who, by learning from the mistakes of others, steers clear of the rocks and shoals were so many have perished.

"In England, the man is made by his business." In that nation, a guy is not considered a gentleman if he works as a mechanic or other type of laborer. The Duke of Wellington

questioned me about
General Tom Thumb's
parents' line of work
during my first appearance
before Queen Victoria.

I responded, "His father is
a carpenter.

"Oh! He was a gentleman,
I'd heard "His Grace's
reaction was.

In this Republican nation, the man controls the economy. He may be a gentleman whether he is a blacksmith, a shoemaker, a farmer, a banker, or a lawyer as long as his profession is lawful. Therefore, any "legal" business is a double blessing because it benefits both the person running it and others. The farmer provides for his own family's necessities, but he also helps the merchant or mechanic who requires his farm's goods. The farmer, the clergyman, and others who are unable to sew their own clothing benefit from the tailor's services in addition to making a living. However, many of these classes may consist of gentlemen.

The main goal should be to outperform everyone else in the field.

The soon-to-be graduated college student said to the senior lawyer:

"My choice of profession is still up in the air. Is your profession already full?"

The amusing and accurate response was, "The basement is rather packed, but there is plenty of room up-stairs."

In the upper storey, there is no profession, trade, or calling that is overcrowded. Wherever you locate the most honorable and wisest businessman or banker, or the greatest doctor, lawyer, or clergyperson, or the best shoemaker, carpenter, or anything else, you will discover that man is most sought after and always has something to do. Americans as a whole are too superficial; they want to become wealthy quickly and don't always conduct business seriously and thoroughly enough.

However, someone who excels in their field, as long as they have good habits and unquestionable integrity, is guaranteed to attract a lot of business and the wealth that follows naturally. Then make "Excelsior" your personal motto because when you live up to it, there is no such thing as failure.

LEARN SOMETHING VALUE-ADDED

In these times of shifting fortunes, where one may be wealthy now but impoverished tomorrow, every man should insist that his children learn a practical trade or profession so that they will have something concrete to fall back on. Many people who have lost all of their resources due to an unforeseen circumstance could be spared from suffering by this arrangement.

LEAD WITH HOPE, BUT DON'T BE TOO VISIONARY

Since they have too much vision, many people are perpetually locked in poverty. They see every endeavor as a sure success, so they constantly switch from one firm to another,

120

always in trouble, always "under the harrow." The idea of "counting the chickens before they are born" is a mistake that dates back a long time, yet it does not appear to get better with time.

DON'T DISTRIBUTE YOUR POWERS

Engage in only one type of business and stay committed to it until you are successful or until your experience indicates that you should stop. One nail will usually finally be driven home with constant hammering, allowing it to be clinched. A man's mind will continually suggest valuable enhancements when his undivided concentration is focused on just one thing; these suggestions would otherwise escape him if his thinking was split between a dozen distinct topics. Many fortunes have been lost by men because they were juggling too many different jobs at once. The age-old advice to avoid juggling too many projects at once makes sense.

BE SYMPATHETIC

Men should conduct themselves in a methodical manner. A person who follows the rules, assigns tasks a time and location, and completes their work on time will accomplish twice as much work with half the effort as someone who is careless and inefficient. You can find time for leisure activities by implementing systems into all of your transactions, completing tasks one at a time, and keeping appointments on time. In contrast, a person who only completes one task in full before switching to another and doing it in half will have unfinished business and will never know when their day's work is finished because it will never be. All of these principles have a certain upper limit, of course. Because being overly methodical is possible, we must work to maintain the happy medium. For instance, some men and women store things so meticulously that they never find them again. It resembles both Mr. Dickens' "Circumlocution Office" and the "red tape" formality in Washington too much—all theory and little action. The "Astor House" was unquestionably the best hotel in the nation when it originally opened in New York City. The owners had studied hotels extensively in Europe, and they were proud of the rigid system that ran across every aspect of their magnificent facility. When it was twelve o'clock at night and there were several visitors there, one of the owners would remark, "Touch that bell, John," and within two minutes, sixty slaves would enter the hall holding a water-bucket in each hand. The landlord explained to his guests, "This is our fire-bell; it will show you we are pretty secure here and we do everything methodically. This was before the city began using Croton water. But occasionally they went too far with their system. The hotel had fifty waiters on staff at the time, but the landlord felt that he needed all of them because otherwise his "system" would be disrupted. This was during a busy time when the hotel was packed with guests. He hurried downstairs just before dinnertime and exclaimed, "There must be another server; I am one waiter short. What can I do?" By chance, he encountered "Boots," the

Irishman. He instructed Pat to wash his hands and face, put on the white apron, and enter the dining room in five minutes. When Pat finally showed up as expected, the owner instructed him to stand behind these two chairs and serve the men who would be sitting in them. Has Pat ever worked as a waiter? Yes, I am well aware of it, but I have never engaged in it. Like the Irish pilot, the captain once questioned him, "Are you sure you understand what you are doing," thinking he was very off course. Sure, and I am familiar with every rock in the channel, Pat retorted. At that precise moment, the ship slammed into a rock. The pilot added, "Ah! be-jabers, and that is one of 'em. But let's head back to the dining area. "Here, Pat," the landlord continued, "everything is done methodically. Prior to asking what they want to eat next, you must first serve the men each a plate of soup." "Ah! and I understand perfectly the virtues of the system," pat retorted. The visitors entered rather quickly. They were presented with the soup plates. One of Pat's two guys consumed their soup, but the other seemed unimpressed. "Waiter, remove this plate and bring me some fish," he ordered. Pat observed the unfinished soup on the plate and, recalling the landlord's instructions regarding "system," he retorted, "Not till ye have eaten yer supe!" Of fact, that went much beyond the bounds of "system."

SEEK NEWS IN THE PAPERS

Always carry a reliable newspaper with you so that you may stay up to date on world events. Without a newspaper, a person is isolated from the rest of his species. Many significant inventions and advances are being developed in every area of trade in these days of telegraphs and steam, so anyone who doesn't read the newspapers may quickly find themselves and their business left in the dark.

WARNING: "EXTERNAL OPERATIONS"

Men who have amassed wealth may find themselves abruptly in poverty. This frequently results from immaturity, which frequently results from gaming and other harmful behaviors. It frequently happens as a result of a man participating in "outside operations" of some kind. He is informed of a large speculation where he can earn a score of thousands after he becomes wealthy through his genuine firm. His friends frequently compliment him, telling him that he was born lucky and that everything he touches turns to gold. Now, if he loses sight of the fact that his sound financial practices, moral character, and close attention to a venture he understood were what led to his success in life, he will pay attention to the siren sounds. He claims: "I'll provide $20,000 in total. I've been fortunate, and my good fortune will soon bring me back $60,000 in cash." After a few days, it becomes apparent that he needs to invest an additional $10,000; shortly thereafter, he is informed that everything is fine but that he will need an additional $25,000 to ensure a rich harvest. However, before

136

he has a chance to realize
this, the bubble bursts,
causing him to lose everything
he owns. At this point, he
realizes what he should have
known at the outset: that no
matter how successful a man
may be in his own business, If
a guy has a lot of money, he
should invest some of it in
anything that seems to
promise success and would
likely be good for humanity;
nevertheless, the amounts
should be moderate, and a
man should never foolishly risk
his hard-earned fortune by
spending it in areas in which
he has no knowledge.

NOT WITHOUT SECURITY; DO NOT ENDORSE

I believe that no man should ever endorse a note or provide security for another man, whether it be his father or brother, in excess of what he can

138

comfortably lose and not care about, without first taking appropriate precautions. You are retired and relying on your savings when a man worth $20,000 approaches you and says: "I have a booming manufacturing or mercantile business.

You are aware that I am worth $20,000 and owe nothing. If I had $5,000 in cash, however, I could buy a specific batch of goods and double my money in a matter of months. Will you endorse my note for that sum?

He is worth $20,000 to you, so there is no risk in

putting your name on his note. You like to accommodate him, so you do so without taking the precaution of getting security. Soon after, when he shows you the note with your endorsement canceled and informs you—likely in truth—that "he made the profit that he expected by the operation," you consider that you've done a nice deed and feel good about it. The same thing eventually happens again, and you continue to act in the same manner because you have already formed the mental image that it is completely safe to endorse his notes without security.

The issue is that this individual is obtaining

money far too effortlessly. Simply take your note to the bank, have it reduced, and have him collect the money. He receives money for the time being without exerting any effort or causing himself any inconvenience. Mark the outcome now. He sees an opportunity for speculative activity unrelated to his company. Only a $10,000 temporary investment is needed. It will undoubtedly return before the bank note is due. He puts a note for that sum in front of you. You almost robotically sign it. You endorse your friend's notes since you are quite certain that he is trustworthy and reliable.

Unfortunately, the rumor does not materialize as quickly as anticipated, necessitating the discounting of another $10,000 note to replace the previous one when it becomes due. The speculation has proven to be a complete disaster before this note matures, and all the money has been lost. Does the loser inform his endorser friend that he has lost half of his wealth? In no way. He doesn't even acknowledge that he has made any speculation. But now that he's become enthused and the spirit of speculation has gripped him, he "looks for his money where he loses it" like other speculators because he sees others gaining big sums of money

in this way (we hardly ever
hear about the losers). He
tries once more. Endorsing
notes has become a habit
with you; at every defeat,
he obtains your signature
for any sum he desires.
Finally, you learn that both
your friend's and your
possessions have been
gone. It is a terrible thing;
my friend here has
wrecked me, you say, but

147

you should also add, "I have also ruined him." You are overcome with shock and anguish as you speak. He would never have been enticed to leave his legitimate business if you had indicated in the beginning, "I would accommodate you, but I never endorse without taking appropriate security." Then he would not have been able to go beyond the limits of his tether. Therefore, giving individuals access to money too easily is never a good idea because, at the very least, it tempts them to engage in risky speculation. Solomon was right when he said, "He who hates surety is sure."

Let the young guy learn the value of money by working for it as he starts his own firm. When he does recognize its worth, you can assist him get his business off the ground by greasing a few cogs, but keep in mind that men who get money with excessive ease frequently fail. To understand the worth of your first cash, you must

150

earn it via struggle and some sacrifice.

PROMOTE YOUR BUSINESS

More or less, we all rely on the support of the general people. Lawyers, doctors, shoemakers, blacksmiths, artists, showmen, opera stage directors, railroad executives, and college teachers all conduct business with the general public. Those that conduct business with the general public need to take care that their products are worthwhile, real, and satisfying. When you find a product that you know will appeal to your audience and that, once they try it, will make them feel like they got their money's worth, let them know that you have found it. Be sure to publicize it in some way because it is obvious that if a man has an exceptionally good item for sale but nobody knows about it, it will not bring him any money. It would be really foolish not to use this avenue to advertise to the public in a nation like this, where almost everyone reads and newspapers are published and distributed in editions of 5,000 to 200,000. Hundreds of thousands of people may read your advertisement while you are going about your daily business since a newspaper is brought into the home and read by the wife, kids, and the head of the household. Perhaps many others read it while you slept. The entire life concept is "sow" first, then "reap." The farmer works in this manner; he plants his corn and potatoes, scatters his seeds, and then moves on to other tasks until it is time to reap. He never, however, reaps first and then sows. This rule is applicable to all business types, but nowhere more so than in advertising. If a man has the real deal, there is no other way for him to benefit more than through "sowing" to the public in this manner. Of course, he needs to have genuinely solid content that will appeal to his audience;

anything fake will fail
eventually because the
general population is more
informed than many
people think. Men and
women are both
egotistical, and we all
prefer to spend our money
in places where we can get
the maximum value,
therefore we search for
these places.

You might advertise a
phony product and get lots
of people to phone and buy
it at once, but then they'll
call you out as a fraud and
a swindler, and your firm
will eventually fail and
you'll be left in poverty.
This is accurate. Few
people can depend on
random customs without
risk. You all need your

clients to come back and make more purchases. "I have tried advertising and did not succeed, but I have a nice piece," a man stated to me.

I answered, "There could be an exception to the rule, my buddy. How do you advertise, though?"

"I paid $1.50 and had it published three times in a weekly newspaper." Sir, advertising is like learning—"a little is a dangerous thing!" was my response.

The reader of a newspaper "does not see the first mention of an ordinary advertisement; the second insertion he sees, but does not read; the third insertion he reads; the fourth insertion he looks at the price; the fifth insertion he speaks of it to his wife; the sixth insertion he is ready to purchase; and the seventh insertion he purchases," according to a French writer. Your goal in advertising is to convey to

the public what you have
to offer, and if you lack the
courage to continue
advertising until you have
done so, all of your
advertising expenses will
be lost. You are similar to
the person who claimed
that if the other person
gave him ten cents, he
would save the other
person a dollar. The man
remarked in amazement,

"How can I help you so much for such a modest amount?" "I had every intention of becoming drunk when I woke up this morning (the guy hiccuped), and despite spending my one and only dollar to do it, I can't quite seem to pull it off. More whiskey costing ten cents would suffice, and by doing so, I would be able to recoup the dollar already spent."

In order to avoid losing the money spent on advertising, a guy who advertises at all must continue doing so until the public is aware of who he is, what he does, and what his business is.

164

Some individuals have a
special aptitude for
creating eye-catching
advertisements that will
grab the reader's attention
right away. Of course, the
marketer benefits greatly
from this fact. Sometimes
a person gains notoriety
through a distinctive sign
or an intriguing display in
his window. Recently, I

noticed a swing sign
overhanging the sidewalk
in front of a store with the
words in plain letters,

**DON'T READ THE
OTHER SIDE**"

Of course, I did, and
everyone else did, and I
discovered that the man
had achieved complete
independence by first

166

drawing consumers to his firm in that manner and then effectively utilizing them later.

Because he believed it would serve as a good advertisement for him, Genin, the hatter, paid $225 for the first Jenny Lind ticket at auction. The auctioneer at Castle Garden asked, "Who is the bidder?" as he slammed that ticket to the ground. The reply was "Genin, the hatter." Thousands of individuals from Fifth Avenue and far-off cities in the highest social classes were present. They cried out, "Who is 'Genin,' the hatter? They had never before heard of him. Five to ten million people read the news that the tickets were sold at auction the following morning after it had been reported in newspapers and on the telegraph from Maine to Texas. Twenty thousand dollars or so were spent on Jenny Lind's first concert, and "Genin, the hatter" paid two hundred and twenty-five dollars for the one ticket that was sold. Men all around the nation

unconsciously removed
their hats to see if they
were wearing "Genin"
hats. In a town in Iowa, it
was discovered that among
the crowd gathered around
the post office, one man
was wearing a "Genin" hat,
which he proudly
displayed despite the fact
that it was worn out and
barely worth two cents.
You have a real "Genin'

hat," one man shouted, "what a lucky fellow you are. Hold onto that hat; it will become a priceless heirloom in your family, suggested another man. Another individual in the audience, who appeared to be envious of the owner of this luck, chimed in, "Come, give us all a chance; put it up for auction!" He did, and it went for $9.50 when it was offered as a souvenir! What were the repercussions for Mr. Genin? For the first six years, he sold 10,000 more hats annually. Ninety percent of his customers undoubtedly bought from him out of curiosity, and many of them became regular customers after discovering that he gave

172

them value for their money. They were initially drawn in by this creative advertisement, and after reading a solid article, they returned.

Now, I'm not advocating that everyone promote like Mr. Genin did. The possibilities are that the sheriff will do it for him one day if he doesn't publicize his stuff for sale, in my opinion. I also do not mandate that anyone use "printers' ink" or advertise in a newspaper. On the other hand, despite the fact that this piece is generally necessary, there are other ways that doctors, priests, and occasionally even lawyers, can effectively communicate with the

public. However, it is clear
that they must be
recognized in some form if
they are to receive
assistance.

BE HUMAN AND GRATEFUL TO YOUR CUSTOMERS

The best capital ever used in business was civility and politeness. If you or your employees treat your customers rudely, large stores, gilded signs, and flamboyant marketing will all be ineffective. The truth is that a man will receive patronage that is more generous the more kind and liberal he is. Like produces like. Long-term success is typically best achieved by the person who offers the most things of a comparable quality for the least amount of money while yet keeping a profit for himself. This takes us to the golden rule: "Do unto others as you would have them do unto you." If you follow this advice, people will treat you better than if you consistently act as though you only want the best deal possible. Men who aggressively haggle with their clients while acting as though they never plan to see them again won't be taken in. They won't ever again interact with them as clients.

People dislike paying and receiving a kick in the pants.

When a man was in the lecture room, one of the ushers in my museum once informed me he planned to whip him as soon as he left.

What for? I questioned.

The usher answered, "He stated I wasn't a gentleman.

He pays for that, so don't worry about it, I retorted, "and you won't convince him you're a gentlemen by whipping him. I can't risk losing a client. If you scold him, he won't go to the Museum ever again and will persuade his friends to go somewhere else to have fun instead. As you can see, I would lose badly.

But he insulted me," the usher mumbled.

I agreed, adding, "Exactly, and if he owned the Museum, and you had paid him for the opportunity of visiting it, and he had insulted you, there may be some justification in your resentment of it. However, in this case, he is the one who pays, while we receive, so you must put up with his rudeness.

This is surely the correct policy, my usher said with a chuckle, but he added that he shouldn't object to a raise in pay if he was anticipated to be used improperly to advance my interests.

THINK CHARITABLY

Men should be charitable, without a doubt, as it is

both their responsibility
and their pleasure. Even
so, if you don't have any
other incentives, you'll
discover that the liberal
man will get favors while
the vile, heartless miser
will be shunned.

There are those who scatter
and yet increase, and there
are those who withhold
more than is necessary, yet

184

this leads to poverty, according to Solomon. Of course, genuine charity comes only from the heart.

Helping people who are prepared to assist themselves is the best form of charity. Promiscuous almsgiving is wrong in every way because it doesn't consider the applicant's merit. The kind that "scatters and yet increases" is finding and silently helping individuals who are suffering for themselves. Do not, however, adopt the habit of delivering a prayer or benediction to the hungry in place of a potato or a piece of bread, as some people do. Making Christians is simpler when

186

one is full than when one is
not.

AVOID BLAB

Some men make the stupid
habit of divulging their
trade secrets. If they are
successful, they like
sharing their secrets with
their neighbors. This
results in little gain and
frequently great loss. Don't

187

mention your earnings, hopes, expectations, or intentions. As well as in person, this should also apply in writing. Never write a letter or destroy one, Mephistopheles is forced to say by Goethe. Letters are something that businessmen must write, but they must be careful with their content. If you are losing money, exercise

extra caution and don't
disclose it to others
because you risk damaging
your reputation.

DON'T LOSE YOUR INTEGRITY

It is more valuable than rubies or diamonds. Get money, get it honestly if you can, but get money, the old miser told his sons. In addition to being horribly wicked, this advice embodied stupidity: It was nearly saying, "If you have trouble getting money legitimately, you

190

can easily get it dishonestly. Put it in that manner." Stupid fool! not knowing that earning money dishonestly is the hardest thing in life! Not understanding that no man can be dishonest without soon being found out and that when his lack of principles is discovered, nearly every door to success is closed against him for good. Our prisons are full of men who tried to follow this advice. The general public rightfully avoids anyone whose integrity is questioned. No one of us dares to deal with a man, no matter how courteous, pleasant, and accommodating he may be, if we suspect "false weights and measures." Strict honesty is the key to

success in life—not just
financially, but in every
other way as well. Integrity
of character without
compromise is priceless.
No amount of money,
houses, or lands can buy
the peace and joy it brings
to its owner—peace and
joy that can only be
attained with it. A man
with a reputation for being
absolutely honest may be

extremely poor, but he has access to everyone in the community's funds because everyone knows that if he promises to repay what he borrows, he will never let them down. Therefore, everyone will discover that Dr. Franklin's maxim, "Honesty is the best policy," can never fail to be true if a man had no higher motivation for

being honest than
selfishness.

Being successful is not
always equated with being
wealthy. There are many
honest and pious people
who are richer and happier
than any man can ever be
while he violates the
higher laws of his being,
but there are also many
honest and pious people

who have never owned as much money as some rich people waste in a week.

Money itself, when used properly, is not only a "handy thing to have in the house," but it also provides the satisfaction of blessing our race by allowing its possessor to increase the scope of human happiness and human influence.

There is no doubt that an excessive love of money may be and is "the root of all evil," but money itself is not only a "handy thing to have in the house." The desire for wealth is almost universal, and no one can argue that it is not admirable as long as the owner accepts their obligations and uses their wealth to benefit humanity.

The history of making money, or commerce, is the history of civilization, and wherever trade has thrived the most, art and science have also yielded the highest rewards. Actually, those who make money are generally the ones who benefit our race. We owe a great deal of gratitude to them for the academies, universities, and churches that serve as our institutions of higher learning and the arts. The fact that there are occasionally misers who hoard money solely for the purpose of hoarding and who have no greater aim than to seize everything that is within their grasp is not an argument against the desire for, or the possession of, riches. There are occasionally misers among those who make money, just as there are occasionally hypocrites in religion and populists in politics. But these are merely the exceptions to the rule. But when we encounter such an annoyance and roadblock as a miser in this nation, we are grateful that there are no primogeniture rules in place here and that, in the course of nature, the hoarded dust will eventually be dispersed for the good of humanity. Therefore, I sincerely advise everyone, male and female, to make money honestly rather than dishonestly because Shakespeare was right when he said, "He that

wants money, means, and
content is without three
good friends."